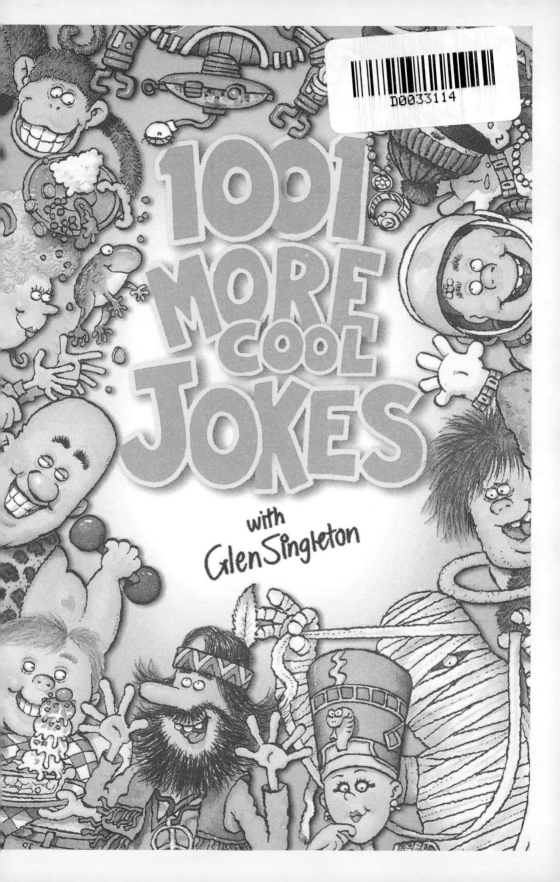

1001 MORE COOL JOKES

with

Glen Singleton

Published by
Hinkler Books Pty. Ltd.
17-23 Redwood Drive
Dingley Victoria 3172
www.hinklerbooks.com

ISBN: 1 865 15 441 5

Publisher's thanks to Barb Whiter for compiling the jokes.
Cover design & illustrations by Glen Singleton.

Printed and bound in Australia.

CONTENTS

Animals

1 **W**hat is a polygon?

A dead parrot.

2 **W**hat do owls sing when it's raining?

Too wet to woo.

3 **W**hat has 500 pairs of sneakers, a ball, and two hoops?

A centipede basketball team.

Obviously a very rich elephant who chose not to eat his peanuts

PEANUTS

PEANUTS

4 **W**hy do elephants never get rich?

Because they work for peanuts.

AAHRRR

AARRRR

5 **W**hat is striped and bouncy?

A tiger on a pogo stick.

6 **W**hen do kangaroos celebrate their birthdays?

During leap year.

7 **W**hat did one bee say to her nosy neighbor bee?

"Mind your own bees' nest!"

8 **W**hat do you do with a mouse that squeaks?

You oil him.

9 **W**ho was the first deer astronaut?

Buck Rogers.

10 **W**here does a pig go to pawn his watch?

A ham hock shop.

11 **W**hat happens when a chimpanzee sprains his ankle?

He gets a monkey wrench.

12 **W**hat happened to the male bee that fell in love?

He got stuck on his honey.

13 **W**hat flies through the jungle singing operetta?

The parrots of Penzance.

14 **W**hat's the best way to catch a monkey?

Climb a tree and act like a banana.

15 **W**hat do you get if you cross a tiger with a sheep?

A striped sweater.

16 **W**hat do you get if you cross a tiger with a snowman?

Frostbite.

17 **W**hat do you get if you cross a tiger with a kangaroo?

A striped jumper.

18 **W**hat is white, lives in the Himalayas and lays eggs?

The Abominable Snow Chicken.

19 **W**hat do you call a crazy chicken?

A cuckoo cluck.

20 **W**hat do you get if you cross Bambi with a ghost?

Bamboo.

21 **O**n which side does an eagle have most of its feathers?

On the outside.

Definitely NOT a crate of ducks!

22 **W**hat do you call a crate of ducks?

A box of quackers.

23 **W**hat's the difference between a mouse and an elephant?

About a ton.

The luckiest bug in the pond

24 **W**hat happened to two frogs that caught the same bug at the same time?

They got tongue-tied.

25 **W**hat's the best way to face a timid mouse?

Lie down in front of its mouse hole and cover your nose with cheese spread!

26 **W**hat do termites eat for dessert?

Toothpicks.

27 **W**hat time is it when an elephant climbs into your bed?

Time to get a new bed.

28 **W**hat kind of key doesn't unlock any doors?

A donkey.

29 **W**hat do you get if you cross a hyena with a bouillon cube?

An animal that makes a laughing stock of itself.

30 **W**hat do you get if you pour hot water down a rabbit hole?

Hot cross bunnies.

31 **W**hy did the man cross a chicken with an octopus?

So everyone in his family could have a leg each.

32 **W**hat has six legs and can fly long distances?

Three swallows.

33 **W**hat do you get if you cross a pig with a zebra?

Striped sausages.

34 **W**hat do vultures always have for dinner?
Leftovers.

35 **W**hat do you get if you cross a duck with a firework?
A fire-quacker.

36 **W**hat do patriotic monkeys wave on July 4th?
Star spangled bananas.

37 **W**hy do buffaloes always travel in herds?
Because they're afraid of getting mugged by elephants.

38 **W**here do sharks shop?
The fish market.

39 **W**hat do you call the autobiography of a shark?
A fishy story.

40 **W**hy don't baby birds smile?

Would you smile if your mother fed you worms all day?

41 **W**hat do you call a travelling mosquito?

An itch hiker.

42 **W**hat is a duck's favorite T.V. show?

The feather forecast.

43 **W**hat did the rabbit give his girlfriend when they got engaged?

A 24-carrot ring.

44 **W**hat do you do if your chicken feels sick?

Give her an eggs-ray.

45 **W**hat sort of music is played most in the jungle?

Snake, rattle, and roll.

46 **W**here do tadpoles change into frogs?

The croakroom.

47 **W**hat's the tallest yellow flower in the world?

A giraffodil.

48 **W**hat do elephants take when they can't sleep?

Trunkquilisers.

49 **W**hich animals were the last to leave the ark?

The elephants – they were packing their trunks.

50 **H**ow do ducks play tennis?

With a quacket.

51 **W**hat sort of a bird steals from banks?

A robin.

52 **W**hy do bears have fur coats?

Because they can't get plastic raincoats in their size!

53 **W**hat would you get if you crossed a hunting dog with a journalist?

A news hound.

54 **W**here is the hottest place in the jungle?

Under a gorilla.

55 **W**hat do you call a bull taking a nap?

A bull dozer.

56 **W**hat is the biggest ant in the world?

An eleph-ant.

57 **W**hat's even bigger than that?

A gi-ant!

58 **H**ow many ants are needed to fill an apartment?

Ten-ants.

59 **W**here do ants eat?

A restaur-ant.

60 **W**hat bird is always out of breath?

A puffin.

61 **W**hat's the difference between a gym teacher and a duck?

One goes quick on its legs and the other goes quack on its legs!

62   **H**ow do fireflies start a race?

Ready, set, glow!

63   **W**hat do you get if you cross a leopard with a watchdog?

A terrified postman.

64   **W**hy were flies playing football in a saucer?

They were playing for the cup.

65   **W**hat do you get if you cross a bottle of water with an electric eel?

A bit of a shock!

66   **W**hat do you get if you cross an eel with a shopper?

A crazy customer.

67 **W**hat do you call a neurotic octopus?

A crazy, mixed-up squid.

68 **W**hat do you call a bird that lives underground?

A mynah bird.

69 **W**hich birds steal the soap from the bath?

Robber ducks.

70 **H**ow do we know that owls are smarter than chickens?

Have you ever heard of Kentucky-fried owl?

71 **W**hat do tigers wear in bed?

Striped pajamas!

72 **W**hen is a lion not a lion?

When he turns into his den.

73 **W**hat does an octopus wear when it's cold?

A coat of arms.

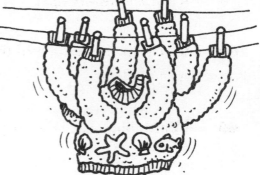

WASH DAY AT THE OCTOPUS' PLACE

74 **W**hat's slimy, tastes of raspberry, is wobbly and lives in the sea?

A red jellyfish.

75 **W**hat is a parrot's favorite game?

Hide and speak.

76 **W**hat do parrots eat?

Polyfilla.

77 What do you call a Scottish parrot?

A Macaw.

78 What do you get if you cross a parrot with a shark?

A bird that will talk your ear off!

79 What do you get if you cross an electric eel with a sponge?

Shock absorbers.

80 What's an eel's favorite song?

"Slip Sliding Away."

81 What do you get if you cross a frog with a small dog?

A croaker spaniel.

82 What is a narrow squeak?

A thin mouse!

83 **W**hat's small, squeaks, and hangs out in caves?

Stalagmice.

84 **W**hat do you call a mouse that can pick up a monster?

Sir.

WATCH IT BIG BOY!

85 **W**hat happens when ducks fly upside-down?

They quack up.

86 **H**ow can you tell the difference between a rabbit and a monster?

Ever tried getting a monster into a rabbit hutch?

87 **W**hat happened when the owl lost his voice?

He didn't give a hoot.

88 **W**hat goes "dot, dot, dash, squeak?"

Mouse code.

An owl with laryngitis

89 **W**hat do you get if you cross a parrot with a woodpecker?

A bird that talks in Morse code.

90 **I**f you cross a witch's cat with Father Christmas, what do you get?

Santa Claws.

91 **N**ow you see it, now you don't. What could you be looking at?

A black cat walking over a zebra crossing!

92 **W**hat do you call a deer with no eyes?

No idea.

93 **W**here do Noah's
bees live?

In ark hives.

94 **W**hat's another
name for a clever
duck?

A wise quacker!

95 **W**hat is a termite's
favorite breakfast?

Oak-meal.

96 **W**hat's the
difference between
a mosquito and a
fly?

*Try zipping up a
mosquito!*

97 **W**hy did the insects drop the centipede from their
football team?

He took too long to put on his shoes!

98 **W**hat did the lion say to his cubs when he taught
them to hunt?

*Don't walk across the road until you see the zebra
crossing.*

99 **W**hat do lions say before they go out hunting for food?

Let us prey.

100 **W**hat flies around your light at night and can bite off your head?

A tiger moth.

101 **W**hat's a lion's favorite food?

Baked beings.

102 **W**hat does a lion brush his mane with?

A catacomb.

103 **W**hat happened when the lion ate the comedian?

He felt funny.

104 **H**ow can you get a set of teeth put in for free?

Tease a lion.

105 **H**ow does a lion say hi! to other animals?

Pleased to eat you!

106 **W**hat's the difference between a tiger and a lion?

A tiger has the mane part missing.

107 **W**hat happened to the leopard who took four baths every day?

Within a week he was spotless.

108 **W**hy are tigers and sergeants in the army alike?

They both wear the stripes.

109 **W**hy did the lion feel sick after he'd eaten the priest?

Because it's hard to keep a good man down.

110 **W**hat do you call a lion wearing a hat?

A dandy lion.

111 **W**hat did the lioness say to the cub chasing the hunter?

Stop playing with your food.

112 **W**hat did the croaking frog say to her friend?

I think I've got a person in my throat.

113 **W**hat did the termite say when she saw that her friends had completely eaten a chair?

Wooden you know it!

Computers

114 **H**ow do computers make sweaters?
On the interknit.

115 **W**hy was the
computer in pain?
*It had a slipped
disk!*

116 **W**hy was the
computer so thin?
*Because it hadn't
had many bytes!*

117 **W**hy did the cat sit on the computer?
To keep an eye on the mouse.

The cat that made off with the mouse... and the computer

118 **W**hat sits in the middle of the world wide web?

A very, very big spider.

119 **W**hy did the vampire bite a computer?

Because he wanted to get on the interneck.

120 **"D**o you turn on your computer with your left hand or your right hand?"

"My right hand."

"Amazing! Most people have to use the on/off switch!"

121 **"I**s this the computer help line?

Every time I log on as a Seven Dwarf, my computer screen goes snow white."

122 **C**ustomer: "I cleaned my computer, and now it doesn't work."

Repairman: *"What did you clean it with?"*

Customer: "Soap and water."

Repairman: *"Water's not meant to be used on a computer!"*

Customer: "Oh, I bet it wasn't the water that caused the problem. It was when I put it in the dryer!"

123 **D**id you hear about the monkey who left bits of his lunch all over the computer?

His dad went bananas.

124 **H**ow do you stop your laptop batteries from running out?

Hide their sneakers!

125 **"I** bought this computer yesterday and I found a twig in the disk drive!"

"I'm sorry, Sir. You'll have to speak to the branch manager."

126 **"I**'ve been on my computer all night!"

"Don't you think you'd be more comfortable on a bed, like everyone else?"

127 **"M**om, Mom, Dad's broken my computer!"

"How did he do that?"

"I dropped it on his head!"

Dinosaurs

128 **W**hy do dinosaurs have wrinkles in their knees?

Because they've stayed in the bath too long.

129 **W**hy did the dinosaur fall out of a palm tree?

Because a hippopotamus pushed him out.

130 **W**hat do you get if you cross a dinosaur with a werewolf?

Who knows, but I wouldn't want to be within a thousand miles of it when the moon is full!

131 **W**hy do dinosaurs have flat feet?

Because they don't wear sneakers.

132 **H**ow do you tell if a dinosaur comes to visit?

He parks his tricycle outside.

133 **W**hy did the dinosaur lie on his back in the water and stick his feet up?

So people could see he wasn't a bar of soap.

134 **W**hy do dinosaurs wear glasses?

So they don't step on other dinosaurs.

135 **W**hat's red on the outside and green inside?

A dinosaur wearing red pajamas.

136 **W**hat do you get if you cross a dinosaur with a kangaroo?

A huge animal that causes earthquakes wherever it hops.

137 **W**hat do you get if you cross a dinosaur with a termite?

A huge bug that eats big buildings for breakfast!

Doctor, Doctor

138 Doctor, Doctor, I have a carrot growing out of my ear.

Amazing! How could that have happened?

I don't understand it. I planted cabbages in there!

139 Doctor, Doctor, I've spent so long at my computer that I now see double.

Well, walk around with one eye shut.

140 Doctor, Doctor, can I have a bottle of aspirin and a pot of glue?

Why?

Because I've got a splitting headache!

Oh my.... Now that is a nasty migraine..!

141   Doctor, Doctor, my little brother thinks he's a computer.

Well bring him in so I can cure him.

I can't. I need to use him to finish my homework!

142   Doctor, Doctor, should I surf the Internet on an empty stomach?

No, you should do it on a computer.

143   Doctor, Doctor, my girlfriend thinks she's a duck.

You'd better bring her in to see my right away.

I can't. She's already flown south for the winter.

144   Doctor, Doctor, I think I've been bitten by a vampire.

Drink this glass of water.

Will it make me better?

No, but I'll be able to see if your neck leaks!

145 **D**octor, Doctor, my son has swallowed my pen. What should I do?

Use a pencil until I get there.

146 **D**octor, Doctor, I think I'm a bell.

Take these, and if they don't help, give me a ring!

147 **D**octor, Doctor, I've got gas! Can you give me something?

Yes! Here's my car.

148 **D**octor, Doctor, I keep thinking I'm a dog.

Sit on the couch and we'll talk about it.

But I'm not allowed on the furniture!

149 **D**octor, Doctor, I think I'm a bridge.

What's come over you?

Oh, two cars, a large truck, and a bus.

150 **D**octor, Doctor, can I have a second opinion?

Of course, come back tomorrow.

151 **D**octor, Doctor, when I press with my finger here . . .

it hurts, and here . . .

it hurts, and here . . .

and here!

What do you think is wrong with me?

Your finger's broken!

152 **D**octor, Doctor, you have to help me out!

That's easy. Which way did you come in?

153 **D**octor, Doctor, I've swallowed my harmonica!

Well, it's a good thing you don't play the piano.

154 **D**octor, Doctor, I keep getting a pain in the eye when I drink coffee.

Have you tried taking the spoon out of the cup before you drink?

155 **D**octor, Doctor, I feel like a spoon!

Well, sit down and don't stir!

156 **D**octor, Doctor, I think I need glasses.

You certainly do. You've just walked into a restaurant!

157 **D**octor, Doctor, I've just swallowed a pen.

Well, sit down and write your name!

158 **D**octor, Doctor, I feel like a dog.

Sit!

159 **D**octor, Doctor, I feel like an apple.

We must get to the core of this!

160 **D**octor, Doctor, I feel like a sheep.

That's baaaaaaaaaaad!

161 **D**octor, Doctor, I'm becoming invisible.

Yes, I can see you're not all there!

162 **D**octor, Doctor, will this ointment clear up my spots?

I never make rash promises!

163 **D**octor, Doctor, everyone keeps throwing me in the garbage.

Don't talk rubbish!

164 **D**octor, Doctor, I'm boiling up!

Just simmer down!

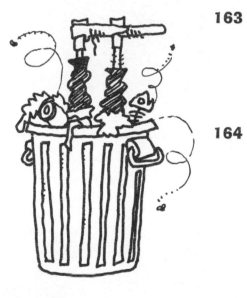

165 **D**octor, Doctor, I feel like a needle.

I see your point!

166 **D**octor, Doctor, how can I cure my sleepwalking?

Sprinkle thumb tacks on your bedroom floor!

A GUARANTEED CURE FOR SLEEPWALKING

167 **D**octor, Doctor, I feel like a racehorse.

Take one of these every four laps!

168 **D**octor, Doctor, I feel like a bee.

Buzz off. I'm busy!

169 **D**octor, Doctor, I'm a burglar!

Have you taken anything for it?

170 Doctor, Doctor, I keep seeing an insect spinning.

Don't worry. It's just a bug that's going around.

171 Doctor, Doctor, how can I stop my nose from running?

Stick your foot out and trip it up!

172 Doctor, Doctor, I'm having trouble with my breathing.

I'll give you something that will soon put a stop to that!

173 Doctor, Doctor, I tend to flush a lot.

Don't worry. It's just a chain reaction.

174 Doctor, Doctor, everyone thinks I'm a liar.

Well, that's hard to believe!

175 Doctor, Doctor, my baby looks just like his father.

Never mind – just as long as he's healthy.

176 **D**octor, Doctor, what did the x-ray of my head show?

Absolutely nothing!

177 **D**octor, Doctor, I think I'm a python.

You can't get around me that easy, you know!

178 **D**octor, Doctor, I keep thinking I'm a mosquito.

Go away, sucker!

179 **D**octor, Doctor, I think I'm a moth.

So why did you come around then?

Well, I saw this light at the window . . .

180 **D**octor, Doctor, I think I'm a moth.

Get out of the way. You're in my light!

181 **D**octor, Doctor, I keep thinking I'm a spider.

What a web of lies!

182 Doctor, Doctor, I think I'm a snail.

Don't worry. We'll soon have you out of your shell.

183 Doctor, Doctor, I think I'm a calculator.

Great, can you help me with my accounts please?

184 Doctor, Doctor, I keep painting myself gold.

Don't worry. It's just a gilt complex.

185 Doctor, Doctor, I think I'm a rubber band.

Why don't you stretch yourself out on the couch there, and tell me all about it?

186 Doctor, Doctor, I feel like a pair of curtains.

Oh, pull yourself together!

187 Doctor, Doctor, everyone keeps ignoring me.

Next please!

188 Doctor, Doctor, I keep thinking I'm a computer.

My goodness, you'd better come to my office right away!

I can't. My power cable won't reach that far!

189 Doctor, Doctor, I don't think I'm a computer any more.

Now I think I'm a desk.

You're just letting things get on top of you.

190 Doctor, Doctor, I think I'm a computer.

How long have you felt like this?

Ever since I was switched on!

191 Doctor, Doctor, I keep thinking there's two of me.

One at a time please!

192 Doctor, Doctor, some days I feel like a tipi and other days I feel like a wigwam.

Relax, you're too tents!

193 Doctor, Doctor, my little boy has just swallowed a roll of film.

Hmmm. Let's hope nothing develops!

194 Doctor, Doctor, I can't get to sleep.

Sit on the edge of the bed, and you'll soon drop off.

195 Doctor, Doctor, I feel like a pack of cards.

I'll deal with you later!

196 Doctor, Doctor, I snore so loudly that I keep myself awake.

Sleep in another room, then.

197 Doctor, Doctor, I have a split personality.

Well, you'd better both sit down, then.

198 Doctor, Doctor, my sister keeps thinking she's invisible.

Which sister?

199 Doctor, Doctor, I think I'm a yo-yo.

You're stringing me along!

200 Doctor, Doctor, I keep thinking I'm a vampire.

Necks, please!

201 Doctor, Doctor, I swallowed a bone.

Are you choking?

No, I really did!

202 Doctor, Doctor, I dream there are zombies under my bed. What can I do?

Saw the legs off your bed.

203 Doctor, Doctor, I think I'm a drill.

How boring for you!

204 **D**octor, Doctor, I think I'm an electric eel.

That's shocking!

205 **D**octor, Doctor, I think I'm a nit.

Will you get out of my hair?

Some patients just get in your hair

206 **D**octor, Doctor, I've broken my arm in two places.

Well, don't go back there again.

207 **D**octor, Doctor, I think I'm a butterfly.

Will you say what you mean and stop flitting about!

208 **D**octor, Doctor, I think I'm a frog.

What's wrong with that?

I think I'm going to croak!

CROAK

Oh that's better!

209 **D**octor, Doctor, I think I'm a caterpillar.

Don't worry. You'll soon change.

210 **D**octor, Doctor, my hair keeps falling out. Can you give me something to keep it in?

Sure, here's a paper bag.

211 **D**octor, Doctor, these pills you gave me for B.O...

What's wrong with them?

They keep slipping out from under my arms!

212 **D**octor, Doctor, my husband smells like a fish.

Poor sole!

213 **D**octor, Doctor, my sister thinks she's an elevator.

Well tell her to come in.

I can't, she doesn't stop at this floor!

Jokes about Boys

214 **M**om: *"Why are you scratching Jamie?"*
Jamie: *"Because no one else knows where I itch.*

215 **D**id you hear
about the boy who
wanted to run
away to the
circus?

*He ended up in a
flea circus!*

216 **W**hy did the boy
take an aspirin
after hearing the
werewolf howl?

*Because it gave him
an eerie ache.*

217 **D**id you hear about the boy who saw a witch riding on a broomstick?

He asked *"What are you doing on that?"*

She replied *"My sister has the vacuum cleaner!"*

218 **A** little boy came running into the kitchen.

"Dad, Dad" he said, *"there's a monster at the door with a really ugly face."*

"Tell him you've already got one," said his father!

219 Why was the boy unhappy to win the prize for best costume at the Halloween party?

Because he just came to pick up his little sister!

220 Why did the boy carry a clock and a bird on Halloween?

It was for tick or tweet!

A few too many good turns I feel

221 Did you hear about the dizzy Boy Scout?

He spent all day doing good turns.

222 Boy monster: *"You have a face like a million dollars."*

Girl monster: *"Have I really?"*

Boy monster: *"Sure, it's green and wrinkly!"*

223 What do you get if you cross a zombie with a Boy Scout?

A creature that scares old ladies across the street.

224 How did the invisible boy upset his mother?

He kept appearing.

225 Igor: *"How was that horror movie you saw last night?"*

Dr. Frankenstein: *"Oh, the same old story: Boy meets girl, boy loses girl, boy builds new girl."*

226 Did you hear about the boy who got worried when his nose grew to be 11 inches long?

He thought it might turn into a foot.

227 Did you hear about the little boy who was named after his father?

They called him Dad.

228 Did you hear about the two boys who found themselves in a modern art gallery by mistake?

"Quick," said one. *"Run, before they say we did it!"*

229   **A** boy broke his arm playing football.

After his arm had been put into a cast, he asked the doctor, *"When you take the plaster off, will I be able to play the drums?"*

"Of course you will," said the doctor, reassuringly.

"That's great!" said the boy. *"I've never been able to play before!"*

230   **R**oy: *"They say ignorance is bliss."*

Rita: *"Then you should be the happiest boy in the world!"*

231   **"K**eep that dog out of my garden. It's disgusting!"* a neighbor said to a little boy one day.

The boy went home to his family and told them to stay away from the neighbor's garden because of the bad smell!

232 **D**id you hear about the boy who sat under a cow?

He got a pat on the head.

233 **D**id you hear about the boy who was known as Fog?

He was dense and wet!

234 **B**oys' favorite films

The Fly, Batman, Beetlejuice, The Sting, The Good, The Bug and the Ugly, Spawn, The Frog Prince, Four Webbings and a Funeral, Seven Bats for Seven Brothers.

235 **W**hy did the boy take a pencil to bed?

To draw the curtains!

236 **I**'d tell you another joke about a boy and a pencil, but there's no point.

237 **W**hy did the lazy boy get a job in a bakery?

Because he wanted to loaf around!

238 **A** naughty boy was annoying all the passengers on a plane.

At last, one man could stand it no longer.

"Hey kid," he shouted. *"Why don't you go outside and play?"*

239 **J**ack: *"Mom, all the boys at school call me Big Head."*

Mom: *"Never mind, Dear. Just run down to the grocery store and bring home the big bag of apples in your baseball hat."*

240 **G**ood news: Two boys went out to climb trees.

Bad news: *One of them fell out.*

Good news: A hammock was beneath him.

Bad news: *A rake was beside the hammock.*

Good news: He missed the rake.

Bad news: *He missed the hammock too!*

241 **W**hy did the boy wear five watches?

He liked to have a lot of time on his hands.

242 **D**id you hear about the boy who stole some rhubarb?

He was put into custardy.

243 **T**wo boys camping out in the backyard wanted to know the time, so they started singing at the top of their voices.

Soon, one of the neighbors threw open his window and shouted, *"Hey, cut the noise! Don't you know it's 3 o'clock in the morning?"*

244 **W**hen George left school he was going to be a printer.

All his teachers said he was the right type.

245 **A** boy staying in an old house meets a ghost in the middle of the night.

"I've been walking these corridors for 300 years," says the ghost.

"In that case, can you tell me where the bathroom is?" asks the boy.

246 **A** little boy came home from his first day at kindergarten and said to his mother, *"What's the use of going to school? I can't read, I can't write, and the teacher won't let me talk!"*

247 **D**id you hear about the boy who had to do a project about trains?

He had to keep track of everything.

248 **M**other: *"Who was that on the phone, Sammy?"*

Sammy: *"No one we knew, Mom. Just some man who said it was long distance from Australia, so I told him I knew that already!"*

53

249 A scoutmaster asked a boy in his troop what good deed he had done that day.

"Well," said the Scout. "*My Mom only had one chore left, so I let my brother do it.'*

250 Charlie had a puppy on a leash. He met his brother Jim and said,

"*I just got this puppy for our little brother.*"

"*Really?*" said Jim. "*That was a good trade!*"

Yep... I got the puppy for Bobby... and swapped Dad for this attractive GOLD WRISTWATCH

251 First boy: "*My brother said he'd tell me everything he knows.*"

Second boy: "*He must have been speechless!*"

252 First boy: "*Why is your brother always flying off the handle?*"

Second Boy: "*Because he has a screw loose!*"

253 Peter: "*My brother wants to work badly!*"

Anita: "*As I remember, he usually does!*"

254 **D**an: *"My little brother is a real pain."*

Nan: *"Things could be worse."*

Dan: *"How?"*

Nan: *"He could be twins!"*

255 **F**irst boy: *"Does your brother keep himself clean?"*

Second boy: *"Oh, yes. He takes a bath every month, whether he needs one or not!"*

256 **M**om: *"What are you doing, Son?"*

Boy: *"Writing my brother a letter."*

Mom: *"That's a nice idea, but why are you writing so slowly?"*

Boy: *"Because he can't read very fast!"*

257 **L**ittle brother: *"I'm going to buy a seahorse."*

Big brother: *"Why?"*

Little brother: *"Because I want to play water polo!"*

258 **B**ig brother: *"That planet over there is Mars."*

Little brother: *"Then that other one must be Pa's."*

259 **W**hy did your brother ask your father to sit in the freezer?

Because he wanted an ice pop!

260 **W**hy did the boy wear a life jacket in bed?

Because he slept on a waterbed.

261 **"M**y brother's a professional boxer."

"Heavyweight?"

"No, featherweight. He tickles his opponents to death!"

Feather weight's secret weapon

262 **D**ad: *"Don't be selfish. Let your brother use the sled half the time."*

Son: *"I do, Dad. I use it going down the hill, and he gets to use it coming up the hill!"*

263 **W**hy did your brother go to school at night?

Because he wanted to learn to read in the dark!

264 **D**id you hear about my brother?

He saw a moose's head hanging on a wall and went into the next room to find the rest of it!

265 **M**om: *"Why does your little brother jump up and down before taking his medicine?"*

Boy: *"Because he read the label and it said, 'shake well before using'."*

266 **"M**y brother's been practicing the violin for ten years."

"Is he any good?"

"No, it was nine years before he found out he wasn't supposed to blow!"

267 **L**ittle brother: *"Look, Bro, I have a deck of cards."*

Big brother: *"Big deal!"*

268 My big brother is such a fool. The other day I saw him hitting himself over the head with a hammer.

He was trying to make his head swell so his hat wouldn't fall over his eyes!

269 Was the carpenter's son a chip off the old block?

270 Dad: *"Why is your January progress report so bad?"*

Son: *"Well, you know how it is. Things are always marked down after Christmas!"*

271 Will and Bill were arguing about whose father was stronger.

Will said, *"Well, you know the Pacific Ocean? My dad dug the hole for it."*

Bill wasn't impressed.

"Well, that's nothing. You know the Dead Sea? My father's the one who killed it!"

272 **A** man whose son had just passed his driving test came home one evening and found that the boy had driven into the living room.

"How did you manage that?" he fumed.

"Quite simple, Dad," said the boy. *"I just came in through the kitchen and turned left."*

273 **M**om: *"Haven't you finished filling the salt shaker yet?"*

Son: *"Not yet. It's really hard to get the salt through all those little holes!"*

274 **F**irst witch: *"I took my son to the zoo yesterday."*

Second witch: *"Really? Did they keep him?"*

275 **"W**hy are you crying, Ted?" asked his mom.

"Because my new sneakers hurt," Ted replied.

"That's because you've put them on the wrong feet."

"But they're the only feet I have!"

276 **N**ed: *"What does your dad sell?"*

Ed: *"Salt."*

Ned: *"Well, my dad is a salt seller too."*

Ed: *"Shake!"*

277 "**M**om, can I please change my name right now?" asked Ben.

"Why would you want to do that, Dear?" asked his mom.

"Because Dad says he's going to spank me, as sure as my name's Benjamin!"

278 **D**id you hear about the farmer's boy who hated the country?

He went to the big city and got a job as a shoeshine boy, and so the farmer made hay while the son shone.

279 "**W**illiam," shouted his Mom. "There were two pieces of cake in that pantry last night, and now there's only one. How do you explain that?"

"It was dark in the pantry," said William. "And I didn't see the second piece!"

280 **C**harley: *"My cat likes to drink lemonade."*

Lenny: *"He sure must be a sourpuss!"*

281 **D**id you hear what Dumb Donald did when he offered to paint the garage for his dad?

The instructions said put on three coats, so he put on his jacket, his raincoat, and his overcoat!

282 **D**ad was taking Danny around the museum when they came a cross a magnificent stuffed lion in a case.

"Dad," asked a puzzled Danny.

"How did they shoot the lion without breaking the glass?"

283 **D**ick and Jane were arguing over the breakfast table.

"Oh, you're so stupid!" shouted Dick.

"Dick!" said their father.

"That's quite enough! Now say you're sorry."

"Okay," said Dick. *"Jane, I'm sorry you're stupid."*

284 **M**om: *"How can you practice your trumpet and listen to the radio at the same time?"*

Son: *"Easy, I have two ears!"*

285 **"I** *think my Dad's getting taller,"* said Stan, to his friend.

"What makes you think that?"

"Well, lately I've noticed that his head is sticking through his hair."

286 **J**ohnny collected lots of money from trick-or-treating and he went to the store to buy some chocolate.

"You should give that money to charity," said the shopkeeper.

"No thanks," replied Johnny. *"I'll buy the chocolate. You give the money to charity!"*

287 **"W**illiam, I've been told you're fighting with the boys next door," said his dad.

"Yes Dad," said William. "They're twins, and I needed a way to tell them apart!"

288 **O**ne day Joe's mother said to his father,

"It's such a nice day, I think I'll take Joe to the zoo."

"I wouldn't bother," said his father.

"If they want him, let them come and get him!"

289 **G**eorge knocked on the door of his friend's house.

When his friend's mother answered he asked, "Can Albert come out to play?"

"No," said Albert's mother. "It's too cold."

"Well, then," said George. "Can his soccer ball come out to play?"

290 **B**oy: "Grandpa, do you know how to croak?"

Grandpa: "No, I don't. Why?"

Boy: "Because Daddy says he'll be a rich man when you do!"

291 **W**hy did Matt's bicycle keep falling over?

Because it was two tired.

292 **"M**om," Richard yelled, from the kitchen.

"You know that vase you were always worried I'd break?"

"Yes, Dear. What about it?" asked his mom.

"Well . . . your worries are over."

Mom won't be too mad. . . .
It's only broken into 3 big bits

293 **W**hen Dad came home, he was amazed to see his son sitting on a horse, writing something.

"What are you doing up there?" he asked.

"Well, the teacher told us to write an essay on our favorite animal," replied the boy.

294 **"M**om, *there's a man at the door collecting for the old folk's home,"* said the little boy.

"Shall I give him Grandma?"

295 **"T**he girl who sits beside me in math is very clever," said Alec, to his mother.

"She has enough brains for two."

"Perhaps you'd better think of marriage," said his mom.

296 **A** young boy was helping his dad around the house.

"Son, you're like lightning with that hammer," said the father.

"Really fast, eh, Dad?" said the boy.

"No, Son. You never strike in the same place twice!"

Jokes about Girls

297 What happened when the girl dressed as a spoon left the Halloween party?

No one moved. They couldn't stir without her.

298 First witch: *"My, hasn't your little girl grown!"*

Second witch: *"Yes, she's certainly gruesome."*

You've grown up into the ugliest most gruesome daughter a Mom could ever want!

299 Two girls were having lunch in the schoolyard.

One had an apple, and the other said, *"Watch out for worms!"*

The first girl replied, *"Why should I? They can watch out for themselves!"*

300 **S**ally: *"Can I try on that dress in the window?"*

Salesgirl: *"If you like, but most people use the dressing room."*

301 **T**eacher: *"I'd like you to be very quiet today, girls. I've got a dreadful headache."*

Mary: *"Why don't you do what my mom does when she has a headache?"*

Teacher: *"What's that?"*

Mary: *"She sends us out to play!"*

302 **G**irl: *"Do you like me?"*

Boy: *"As girls go, your fine   and the sooner you go, the better!"*

A FROG

A LILY

303 **W**hat do you call a girl with a frog in her mouth?

Lily!

304 **H**ow does a witch doctor ask a girl to dance?

"Voodoo like to dance with me?"

My... you do have short legs... It feels like I'm dragging you along...

You are!

305 **G**irl: *"I'd buy that dog, but his legs are too short."*

Salesgirl: *"Not really. All four of them touch the floor."*

306 **W**hy did the wizard turn the naughty girl into a mouse?

Because she ratted on him.

307 **W**hat kind of girl does a Mummy take on a date?

Any old girl he can dig up.

308 **F**irst monster: *"That pretty girl over there just rolled her eyes at me."*

Second monster: *"Well, you'd better roll them back. She might need them!"*

309 **W**hat happened to the girl who wore a mouse costume to the Halloween party?

The cat ate her.

310 **S**ome girls who are the picture of health are just painted that way.

311 **W**ho is a vampire likely to fall in love with?

The girl necks door.

312 **T**wo girls were talking in the corridor.

"That boy over there is getting on my nerves," said Clare.

"But he's not even looking at you," replied Megan.

"That's why he's getting on my nerves!" exclaimed Clare.

313 **"A**lice, you never get anything right,"* complained the teacher.

"What kind of job do you think you'll get when you leave school?"

"Well, I want to be a weather girl on T.V." said Alice.

314 **D**id you hear about the girl monster who wasn't pretty and wasn't ugly?

She was pretty ugly!

315 First cannibal: *"Who was that girl I saw you with last night?"*

Second cannibal: *"That was no girl. That was my dinner."*

316 What did the Alaskan schoolboy say to the Alaskan schoolgirl?

What's an ice girl like you doing in a place like this?

317 First girl: *"Whenever I'm down in the dumps, I buy myself a new hat."*

Second girl: *"Oh, so that's where you get them!"*

318 "*Those raisin cookies you sold me yesterday had three cockroaches in them,*" a girl complained over the phone, to the baker.

"*Sorry about that,*" said the baker.

"*If you bring the cockroaches back, I'll give you the three raisins I owe you.*"

319 **W**hy did the girl take a load of hay to bed?

To feed her nightmare.

320 **W**hat is a myth?

A female moth!

321 **W**hat do young female monsters do at parties?

They go around looking for edible bachelors!

322 **H**ave you met the girl who wanted to marry a ghost?

I can't think what possessed her!

323 **W**hy did the small werewolf bite the girl's ankle?

Because he couldn't reach any higher.

324 **A** girl walked into a pet shop and said, *"I'd like a frog for my brother."*

"Sorry," said the shopkeeper. *"We don't do exchanges!"*

325 **D**id you hear about the girl who was so hung up on road safety that she always wore white at night?

Last winter she was knocked down by a snow plow.

326 **D**id you hear about the girl who got engaged and then found out her new fiancé had a wooden leg?

She broke it off, of course.

327 **F**ather: *"I want to take my girl out of this terrible math class."*

Teacher: *"But she's top of the class!"*

Father: *"That's why it must be a terrible class!"*

328 **H**andsome Harry: *"Every time I walk past a girl, she sighs."*

Wisecracking William: *"With relief!"*

329 **W**hy was the Egyptian girl worried?

Because her daddy was a mummy!

330 **B**ill: *"My sister has lovely long hair, all down her back."*

Will: *"Pity it's not on her head!"*

331 **W**hat do you call an amorous insect?

A love bug!

332 **H**ow did the octopus couple walk down the road?

Arm in arm, in arm, in arm, in arm, in arm, in arm, in arm, in arm ...

333 **W**hat do girl snakes write on the bottom of their letters?

With love and hisses!

334 **W**itch: *"When I'm old and ugly, will you still love me?"*

Wizard: *"I do, don't I?"*

335 **W**hat happened when the young wizard met the young witch?

It was love at first fright.

336 **D**id you hear about the vampire who died of a broken heart?

She had loved in vein.

337 **W**hy did the girl cut a hole in her new umbrella?

Because she wanted to tell when it stopped raining!

338 **M**other: *"Why did you put a toad in your brother's bed?"*

Daughter: *"Because I couldn't find a spider."*

339 **W**hy did the girl separate the thread from the needle?

Because the needle had something in its eye.

340 **W**hy did the girl wear a wet shirt all day?

Because the label said "wash and wear".

341 **W**hy did the girl spend two weeks in a revolving door?

Because she was looking for the doorknob.

342 **D**id you hear about the girl who wrote herself a letter but forgot to sign it?

When it arrived, she didn't know who it was from!

343 **B**rother: *"What happened to you?"*

Sister: *"I fell off while I was riding."*

Brother: *"Horseback?"*

Sister: *"I don't know. I'll find out when I get back to the stable."*

344 **F**irst girl: *"Why are you putting your horse's saddle on backward?"*

Second girl: *"How do you know which way I'm going?"*

345 **W**hy doesn't your sister like peanuts?

Have you ever seen a skinny elephant?

346 **W**hat kind of sharks never eat women?

Man-eating sharks!

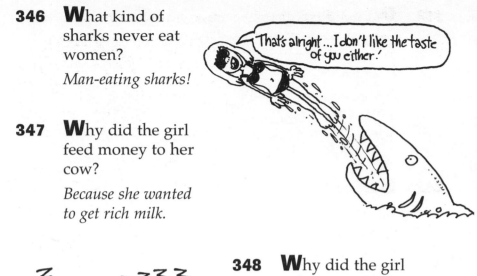

347 **W**hy did the girl feed money to her cow?

Because she wanted to get rich milk.

348 **W**hy did the girl tiptoe past the medicine cabinet?

Because she didn't want to wake the sleeping pills.

349 **M**y sister went on a crash diet.

Is that why she looks a wreck?

350 **W**hy didn't the girl want tickets for a door prize?

Because she already had a door.

351 **W**hy did the girl give cough syrup to the pony?

Because someone told her it was a little horse.

352 **W**hy did the girl have yeast and shoe polish for breakfast?

Because she wanted to rise and shine in the morning!

353 **B**rother: *"Did you just take a shower?"*

Sister: *"Why, is one missing?"*

354 **W**hy did your sister keep running around her bed?

Because she was trying to catch up with her sleep!

355 **M**ary: *"Do you think my sister's pretty?"*

Gary: *"Well, let's just say if you pulled her pigtail, she'd probably say 'oink, oink'!"*

356 **W**hy was your sister fired from her job as an elevator operator?

Because she couldn't remember the route.

357 **D**id you hear about the girl who got her brother a birthday cake but then couldn't figure out how to get the cake in the typewriter to write 'Happy Birthday'?

358 **W**hy did the girl plant birdseed?

Because she wanted to raise canaries!

AHHRRR! WHAT'S THAT?

Oh...it's my toe

359 **W**hy did your sister put her socks on inside out?

Because there was a hole on the outside.

360 **M**y sister is so dim that she thinks a cartoon is something you sing in the car!

361 First vampire: *"I don't think much of your sister's neck!"*

Second vampire: *"Don't worry. Just eat the vegetables."*

362 Did you hear about the time Eddie's sister tried to make a birthday cake?

The candles melted in the oven.

363 Why did the girl jump out of the window?

Because she wanted to try out her new spring suit.

364 Why did the girl take a bicycle to bed?

Because she didn't want to walk in her sleep.

365 What do you call the cannibal who ate her father's sister?

An aunt-eater!

366 **W**hy did the girl put a chicken in a tub of hot water?

Because she wanted the chicken to lay hard-boiled eggs!

367 **L**ucy: *"If you eat any more ice cream, you'll burst."*

Lindy: *"Okay. Pass the ice cream and duck."*

368 **M**other: *"Cathy, get your little sister's hat out of that puddle!"*

Cathy: *"I can't, Mom. She's got it strapped too tight under her chin."*

369 **J**anet: *"What's the difference between a cake and a school bus?"*

Jill: *"I don't know."*

Janet: *"I'm glad I didn't send you to pick up my birthday cake!"*

370 **M**y sister is so dumb that she thinks a buttress is a female goat!

371 Boy: *"Dad! Dad! Come out! My sister's fighting a 10-foot gargoyle with three heads!"*

Dad: *"No, I'm not coming out. She's going to have to learn to look after herself."*

372 First man: *"My girlfriend eats like a bird."*

Second man: *"You mean she hardly eats a thing?"*

First man: *"No, she eats slugs and worms."*

373 Two cannibals were having lunch.

"Your girlfriend makes a great soup," said one to the other.

"Yes!" agreed the first. *"But I'm going to miss her!"*

374 First cannibal: *"My girlfriend's a tough old bird."*

Second cannibal: *"You should have left her in the oven for another half-hour."*

375 "Do you think, Professor, that my girlfriend should take up the piano as a career?"

"No, I think she should put down the lid as a favor!"

376 James: *"I call my girlfriend Peach."*

John: *"Because she's soft and beautiful as a peach?"*

James: *"No, because she's got a heart of stone."*

377 When Wally Witherspoon proposed to his girlfriend, she said,

"I love the simple things in life, but I don't want one of them for a husband!"

378 "I got a gold watch for my girlfriend."

"I wish I could make a trade like that!"

379 "It's a pity you've gone on a hunger strike," said the convict's girlfriend on visiting day.

"Why?" asked the convict.

"Because I've put a file in your cake!"

380 "**M**y girlfriend says that if I don't give up golf, she'll leave me."

"*Say, that's tough, man.*"

"Yeah, I'm going to miss her."

381 **W**hat did the wizard say to his witch girlfriend?

Hello, gore-juice!

382 **M**y girlfriend talks so much that when she goes on vacation, she has to spread suntan lotion on her tongue!

383 **W**hat did the skeleton say to his girlfriend?

I love every bone in your body!

84

384 **W**hat did the undertaker say to his girlfriend?

Em-balmy about you!

385 **I** can't understand why people say my girlfriend's legs look like matchsticks.

They do look like sticks, but they certainly don't match!

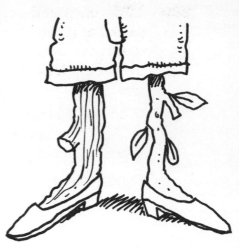

386 **E**very time I take my girlfriend out for a meal, she eats her head off.

She looks better that way.

Oh...
I can't wear these socks out tonight...
They've got a hole in them!

387 **E**mma: *"What a cool pair of odd socks you have on, Jill."*

Jill: *"Yes, and I have another pair just like it at home."*

388 **B**rother: *"Where was Solomon's temple?"*

Sister: *"On either side of his head."*

389 **K**ate: *"I'm going to cross a galaxy with a frog."*

Sharon: *"You'll be sorry. Don't you know what you'll get?"*

Kate: *"No. What?"*

Sharon: *"Star warts!"*

390 Little Susie stood in the department store near the escalator, watching the moving handrail.

"Something wrong, little girl?" asked the security guard.

"Nope," replied Susie. *"I'm just waiting for my chewing gum to come back."*

391 Girl: *"How much is a soft drink?"*

Waitress: *"Fifty cents."*

Girl: *"How much is a refill?"*

Waitress: *"The first is free."*

Girl: *"Well, then, I'll have a refill."*

392 Maria: *"Whatever will Tammy do when she leaves school?*

She's not smart enough to get a job!"

Bonnie: *"She could always be a ventriloquist's dummy."*

393 Teacher: *"Sue, what letter comes after the letter A?"*

Sue: *"The rest of them."*

394 **"M**ary," said her teacher. *"You can't bring that lamb into class. What about the smell?"*

"Oh, that's all right," replied Mary. *"It'll soon get used to it."*

395 **W**hy did Silly Sue throw her guitar away?

Because it had a hole in the middle.

396 **V**isitor: *"You're very quiet, Louise."*

Louise: *"Well, my mom gave me a dollar not to say anything about your red nose."*

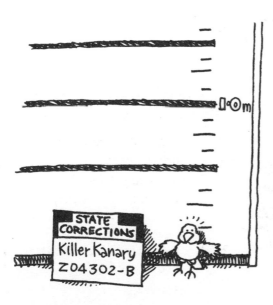

STATE
CORRECTIONS
Killer Kanary
Z04302-B

397 **B**iology teacher: *"What kind of birds do we keep in captivity?"*

Janet: *"Jail birds!"*

398 **J**ane: *"Do you ever do any gardening?"*

Wayne: *"Not often. Why?"*

Jane: *"You look as if you could use some remedial weeding."*

399 **M**ary: *"I've a soft spot for you."*

Harry: *"Ah, really?"*

Mary: *"Yes, in the middle of a swamp!"*

400 **"W**hat shall we play today?" Tanya asked her best friend, Emma.

"Let's play school," said Emma.

"Okay," said Tanya. *"But I'm going to be absent."*

401 **H**elen: *"Mom, do you know what I'm going to give you for your birthday?"*

Mom: *"No, Dear. What?"*

Helen: *"A nice teapot."*

Mom: *"But I already have a nice teapot."*

Helen: *"Not anymore. I just dropped it!"*

402 **M**om: *"Jill, go and play with your whistle outside. Your father can't read his paper."*

Jill: *"Wow, I'm only 8 and I can read it."*

403 Mary's class went to the Natural History Museum.

"Did you enjoy yourself?" asked her mother, when she got home.

"Oh, yes," replied Mary. *"But it was funny going to a dead zoo!"*

404 **"M**rs Johnston, your daughter would be a fine dancer, except for two things."

"What are they?"

"Both feet!"

405 Jane was telling her friend about her vacation in Switzerland. Her friend asked, *"What did you think of the beautiful scenery?"*

"Oh, I couldn't see much," said Jane.

"There were too many mountains in the way."

406 **G**irl to friend: *"I'm sorry, I won't be able to come out tonight. I promised Dad I'd stay in and help him with my homework."*

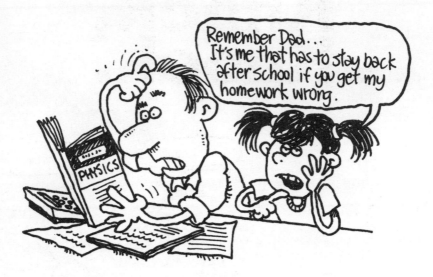

407 **"I** *hope this plane doesn't travel faster than sound,"* said the girl to the flight attendant.

"Why?" asked the flight attendant.

"Because my friend and I want to talk, that's why!"

408 **P**enny: *"Will you join me in a cup of hot chocolate?"*

Mindy: *"Yes, but do you think we'll both fit?"*

Knock, Knock.

409 **K**nock, Knock.
Who's there?
Abba!
Abba who?
Abba banana!

410 **K**nock, Knock.
Who's there?
Abbey!
Abbey who?
Abbey stung me on the nose!

411 **K**nock, Knock.
Who's there?
Abbott!
Abbott who?
Abbott time you opened this door!

412 **K**nock, Knock.
Who's there?
Abe!
Abe who?
Abe C D E F G H . . .

413 **K**nock, Knock.
Who's there?
Abel!
Abel who?
Abel seaman!

414 **K**nock, Knock.
Who's there?
Abyssinia!
Abyssina who?
Abyssinia when I get back!

415 **K**nock, Knock.
Who's there?
Adair!
Adair who?
Adair once, but I'm bald now!

416 **K**nock, Knock.
Who's there?
Adam!
Adam who?
Adam up and tell me the total!

417 **K**nock, Knock.
Who's there?
Arthur!
Arthur who?
Arthur any more at
home like you!

418 **K**nock, Knock.
Who's there?
Baby Owl!
Baby Owl who?
Baby Owl see you
later, maybe I won't!

419 **K**nock, Knock.
Who's there?
Bach!
Bach who?
Bach of chips!

420 **K**nock, Knock.
Who's there?
Bacon!
Bacon who?
Bacon a cake for
your birthday!

421 **K**nock, Knock.
Who's there?
Barbara!
Barbara who?
Barbara black sheep, have you any wool!

422 **K**nock, Knock.
Who's there?
Bernadette!
Bernadette who?
Bernadette my lunch and now I'm starving!

423 **K**nock, Knock.
Who's there?
Olive!
Olive who?
Olive you!

424 **K**nock, knock.
Who's there?
Bee!
Bee who?
Bee careful!

425 **K**nock, Knock.
Who's there?
Beef!
Beef who?
Bee fair now!

426 **K**nock, Knock.
Who's there?
Bella!
Bella who?
Bella bottom trousers!

427 **K**nock, Knock.
Who's there?
Ben!
Ben who?
Ben away a long time!

428 **K**nock, Knock.
Who's there?
Biafra!
Biafra who?
Biafra'id, be very afraid!

429 **K**nock, Knock.
Who's there?
Boxer!
Boxer who?
Boxer tricks!

430 **K**nock, Knock.
Who's there?
Bowl!
Bowl who?
Bowl me over!

431 **K**nock, Knock.
Who's there?
Bridie!
Bridie who?
Bridie light of the
silvery moon!

432 **K**nock, Knock.
Who's there?
Brie!
Brie who?
Brie me my supper!

433 **K**nock, Knock.

Who's there?

Butcher!

Butcher who?

Butcher arms
around me!

434 **K**nock, Knock.

Who's there?

Butcher!

Butcher who?

Butcher left leg
in, your left leg
out!

BUTCHER LEFT LEG IN
AND SHAKE IT
ALL ABOUT

435 **K**nock, Knock.

Who's there?

Butcher!

Butcher who?

Butcher money
where your mouth
is!

436 **K**nock, Knock.

Who's there?

C-2!

C-2 who?

C-2 it that you don't
forget my name next
time!

437 **K**nock, Knock.

Who's there?

Caesar!

Caesar who?

Caesar quickly, before she gets away!

438 **K**nock, Knock.

Who's there?

Caesar!

Caesar who?

Caesar jolly good fellow!

439 **K**nock, Knock.

Who's there?

Carlotta!

Carlotta who?

Carlotta trouble when it breaks down!

440 **K**nock, Knock.

Who's there?

Cantaloupe!

Cantaloupe who?

Cantaloupe with you tonight!

441 **K**nock, Knock.

Who's there?

Canoe!

Canoe who?

Canoe come out
and play with
me?

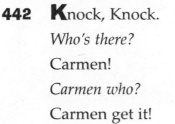

442 **K**nock, Knock.

Who's there?

Carmen!

Carmen who?

Carmen get it!

443 **K**nock, Knock.

Who's there?

Carol!

Carol who?

Carol go if you turn the ignition key!

444 **K**nock, Knock.

Who's there?

Cows!

Cows who?

Cows go
"moo", not
"who"!

445 **K**nock, Knock.
Who's there?
Quacker!
Quacker who?
Quacker 'nother
bad joke and I'm
leaving!

446 **K**nock, Knock.
Who's there?
Nobody!
Nobody who?
Just nobody!

447 **K**nock, Knock.
Who's there?
U-2!
U-2 who?
U-2 can buy a brand
new car for only
$199 a month!

448 **K**nock, Knock.
Who's there?
U-4!
U-4 who?
U-4 me and me for you!

449 **K**nock, Knock.
Who's there?
U-8!
U-8 who?
U-8 my lunch!

450 **K**nock, Knock.
Who's there?
Utah!
Utah who?
Utah the rails and I'll mend the fence!

451 **K**nock, Knock.
Who's there?
Zany!
Zany who?
Zany body home?

452 **K**nock, Knock.
Who's there?
Zeke!
Zeke who?
Zeke and you shall find!

453 **K**nock, Knock.
Who's there?
Zubin!
Zubin who?
Zubin eating garlic again!

454 **K**nock, Knock.
Who's there?
X!
X who?
X-tremely pleased
to meet you!

455 **K**nock, Knock.
Who's there?
X!
X who?
X for breakfast!

Your X are ready!

456 **K**nock, Knock.
Who's there?
Xavier!
Xavier who?
Xavier money for a
rainy day!

457 **K**nock, Knock.
Who's there?
Xavier!
Xavier who?
Xavier breath, I'm not
leaving!

I'm allowed to change my mind... So I have! I'm leaving again!

458 **K**nock, Knock.
Who's there?
Xena!
Xena who?
Xena minute!

459 **K**nock, Knock.
Who's there?
Xenia!
Xenia who?
Xenia stealing my candy!

460 **K**nock, Knock.
Who's there?
Jam!
Jam who?
Jam mind, I'm trying to get out!

461 **K**nock, Knock.
Who's there?
James!
James who?
James people play!

462 **K**nock, Knock.
Who's there?
Jaws!
Jaws who?
Jaws truly!

463 **K**nock, Knock.
Who's there?
Jilly!
Jilly who?
Jilly out here, so
let me in!

464 **K**nock, Knock.
Who's there?
Jim!
Jim who?
Jim mind if we
come in!

Hi...
It's JIM here...
and 42 of
my best friends.
Can we come in?

465 **K**nock, Knock.
Who's there?
Jimmy!
Jimmy who?
Jimmy a little kiss on the cheek!

466 **K**nock, Knock.
Who's there?
Gable!
Gable who?
Gable to leap tall buildings in a single bound!

467 **K**nock, Knock.
Who's there?
Jo!
Jo who?
Jo jump in the lake!

468 **K**nock, Knock.
Who's there?
Gary!
Gary who?
Gary on smiling!

Just a happy guy

469 **K**nock, Knock.
Who's there?
Gizza!
Gizza who?
Gizza kiss!

kissy kissy kissy

105

Miscellaneous

470 **"S**o you are distantly related to the family next door, are you?"

"Yes. Their dog is our dog's brother."

471 **"C**harley, why did Farley run through the screen door?" asked Mom.

"Because he wanted to strain himself!"

472 **H**ow do you make a potato puff?

Chase it around the garden.

473 **W**hat vegetable goes well with jacket potatoes?

Button mushrooms.

474 **W**hat jam can't you eat?

A traffic jam!

475 **I**f the Mounties always get their man, what do postmen always get?

Their mail.

These buttons are overcooked

They feel more like mushrooms

476 Why are giraffes good friends to have?

Because they stick their neck out for you.

477 **W**hat do you get when you cross an orange with a squash court?

Orange squash.

478 **"C**an you lend me $1000?"

"I only have $800."

"That's okay. You can owe me the other $200."

479 **S**tatistics say that one in three people is mentally ill.

So check your friends and if two of them seem okay, you're the one.

480 **A**my: *"Did you find your cat?"*

Karen: *"Yes, he was in the refrigerator."*

Amy: *"Goodness, is he okay?"*

Karen: *"Yes, he's cool!"*

481 **W**hat do you get if you cross a worm with a baby goat?

A dirty kid.

482 **W**hy was the glowworm unhappy?

Her children weren't very bright.

483 **W**hat's the hottest letter in the alphabet?

It's 'b', because it makes oil boil!

484 **W**hat's the difference between Santa Claus and a warm dog?

Santa wears the suit, but a dog just pants.

485 **W**hy did the farmer plow his field with a steamroller?

He wanted to grow mashed potatoes.

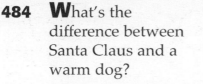

486 **W**e went for a holiday last year to a seaside town.

It was so boring there that the tide went out one day and didn't come back!

487 **W**hat do bees do if they need a ride?

Wait at a buzz stop.

488 **W**hat's green and short and goes camping?

A boy sprout.

489 **W**hat's the difference between a night watchman and a butcher?

One stays awake and the other weighs a steak!

490 **W**hat's green, covered in custard, and sad?

Apple grumble.

491 **W**hat happened when there was a fight in the seafood restaurant?

Two fish got battered.

492 **W**hat's the difference between a young lady and a fresh loaf?

One is a well-bred maid and the other is well-made bread.

493 **W**hat did one tomato say to the one behind him?

Ketchup!

Where all the slow tomatoes end up.

494 **D**uck: "Do you have any lip gloss?"

Storekeeper: *"Yes, of course. Will that be cash or credit?"*

Duck: *"Just put it on my bill."*

Monsters, Witches, Ghosts and Vampires

495 **W**hat do you get if you cross Frankenstein with a hot dog?

Frankenfurterstein.

496 **W**hat monster is the most untidy?

The Loch Mess Monster.

497 **W**hat do you call a monster airline steward?

A fright attendant.

Well, it's definitely been here.... Just look at the mess!

VIEW THE LOCH MESS MONSTER HERE

498 **W**hy did the monster buy an ax?

Because he wanted to get ahead in life.

499 **W**hat is a monster's favorite game?

Hide and Shriek.

500 **W**hat do Italian monsters eat?

Spookgetti.

501 **W**hat do Hungarian monsters eat?

Ghoulash.

502 **W**hat should you take if a monster invites you to dinner?

Someone who can't run as fast as you.

503 What do you think when you see a monster?

"I hope he hasn't seen me!"

504 What do you do with a blue monster?

Try to cheer him up a bit.

505 Why did the monster comedian like playing to skeletons?

Because he knew how to tickle their funny bones.

506 What do you call a monster that comes to collect your laundry?

An undie-taker.

507 If you crossed the Loch Ness monster with a shark, what would you get?

Loch Jaws.

508 What eats its victims two by two?

Noah's Shark.

509 **H**ow do you talk to the Loch Ness monster when he's so far under water?

Drop him a line.

510 **D**uring which age did Mummies live?

The Band-Age.

511 **W**hy was the monster catching centipedes?

He wanted scrambled legs for breakfast.

512 **W**hat does a ghost call his Mom and Dad?

His transparents.

513 **H**ow does Frankenstein eat?

He bolts his food down.

514 **W**hat's a good job for a young monster?

Chop assistant.

515 **W**hat did the metal monster want on his gravestone?

Rust in Peace.

516 **W**here do skeletons keep their money?

In a joint account.

517 **W**hy didn't the skeleton and the monster fight?

The skeleton didn't have the guts.

518 **H**ow many monsters would it take to fill your living room?

How would I know? I'd leave as soon as the first one arrived!

519 **W**hat do you do if a monster rolls his eyes at you?

Just pick them up and roll them back!

520 **W**hy did the young monster take a runner to school in his lunch?

Because he liked fast food.

521 **W**hat do monsters make with cars?
Traffic jam.

522 **W**ho patrols cemeteries at night?
A fright watchman.

523 **W**hat do you have to buy if you invite monsters around for a party?
A new house.

524 **W**hat is a monster's favorite craft?
Tie and die.

525 **W**here do ghosts go to learn to frighten people?
Swooniversity.

526 **W**hat do ghosts use to type letters?
A type-frighter.

527 **W**hat type of horses do monsters ride?
Night mares.

528 **W**hat's the difference between a monster and a cookie?

Have you ever tried to dunk a monster in your milk?

529 **W**hy can't ghosts tell lies?

You can see right through them.

530 **W**hat's a monster's favorite shape?

A vicious circle.

531 **W**hat do ghosts do to keep fit?

They hire an exercisist.

532 **W**here do monsters send their clothes for cleaning?

The dry screamers.

533 **W**hat do monsters like reading in the papers every day?

Their horror-scopes, of course!

534 **W**hat type of music do Mummies prefer?

Wrap music.

535 **W**hat do baby sea monsters play with?

Sea-saws.

536 **W**hat feature do witches love on their computers?

The spell-checker.

537 **W**hy did the ghost go to jail?

For driving without due scare and attention.

538 **W**hat does a Yeti eat for dinner?

An ice burger.

539 **W**hat do you get if you cross King Kong with a frog?

A huge gorilla that can catch a plane with its tongue!

540 **D**oes a monster need a menu while vacationing on a cruise ship?

No, just the passenger list.

541 **W**hat did the monster say when he saw a rush-hour train full of passengers?

Great! A chew-chew train!

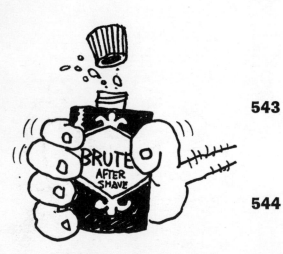

542 **W**hy did the monster eat the lightbulb?

He wanted some light refreshment.

543 **W**hat aftershave do monsters prefer?

Brute.

544 **H**ow do you know there's a monster in your shower?

You can't close the shower curtain.

545   **W**hat should you do if a monster runs through your front door?

Run out the back door.

546   **W**hy did the young monster knit herself three socks?

She grew another foot.

A good use for one of those ODD SOCKS in the back of your drawer.

547   **F**irst monster: *"I've just changed my mind."*

Second monster: *"Does it work better than the old one?"*

548   **O**n which day do monsters eat people?

Chewsday.

Flat batteries in that one!

OLD USED BRAINS

549 What does a monster Mommy say to her kids at dinner time?

Don't speak with someone in your mouth.

550 What's the name of a clever monster?

Frank Einstein.

551 How do you stop a charging monster?

Take away his credit card.

552 How did the monster cure his sore throat?

By gargoyling every day.

553 The police are looking for a monster with one eye.

They should use two!

554 Did you hear about the monster who sent his picture to a lonely hearts club?

They sent it back, saying they weren't that lonely.

555 Did you hear about the monster who lost all his hair in the war?

He lost it in a hair raid.

556 What happened when the ice monster ate a spicy salsa?

He blew his cool.

557 Did you hear what happened to Ray when he met the man-eating monster?

He became an ex-Ray!

558 Why did the monster paint himself in rainbow-colored stripes?

He wanted to hide in a crayon box.

559 Why was the big, hairy, two-headed monster top of the school class?

Because two heads are better than one.

560 **W**hat do ghosts do in the January sales?

Go bargain haunting.

561 **W**hy did the monster eat his music teacher?

His Bach was worse than his bite.

562 **D**id you hear about the little spook who couldn't sleep at night because his brother kept telling him human stories?

563 **D**id the bionic monster have a brother?

No, but he had lots of trans-sisters!

564 **S**mall monster: *"Dad, the dentist wasn't painless like he said he'd be."*

Dad monster: *"Did he hurt you?"*

Small monster: *"No, but he yelled when I bit his finger!"*

565 **W**hat did Dracula call his daughter?

Bloody Mary.

566 **W**hich of the witches' friends eats the fastest?

The goblin.

567 **H**ow does a witch make scrambled eggs?

She holds the pan and gets two friends to make the stove shake with fright.

568 **W**hat do you call a pretty and friendly witch?

A failure.

569 **W**hy do demons and ghouls get on so well?

Because demons are a ghoul's best friend.

570 **H**ow does a skeleton call his friends?

On a telebone.

571 **W**hat do you call a motorcycle belonging to a witch?

A brooooooooooom stick!

572 **W**as Dracula ever married?

No, he was a bat-chelor!

573 **W**hat do you get if you cross a vampire with Al Capone?

A fangster!

574 **W**hy are skeletons usually so calm?

Nothing gets under their skin!

I'm really more the BIKINI ON A BEACHTOWEL sort of girl myself...

575 **W**hat do vampires gamble with?

Stake money!

576 **W**hy do skeletons hate winter?

Because the cold goes right to their bones!

577 **W**hat is red, sweet, and bites people?

A jampire!

578 **W**hat do you call an old and foolish vampire?

A silly old sucker!

a silly old sucker

579 **W**hat story do little witches like to hear at bedtime?

Ghoul deluxe and the three scares!

580 **W**hy do dragons sleep during the day?

So they can fight knights!

BOO! OOOHHH! eeeee!

Try to scare me all you like mate. I was brought up on all that stuff!

581 **W**hat should you say when you meet a ghost?

How do you boo, Sir?

582 **W**hat did the mother ghost say to the baby ghost?

Put your boos and shocks on!

583 **W**hat would
you find on a
haunted beach?
A sand witch!

584 **W**hen do
ghosts usually
appear?
*Just before
someone screams!*

585 **W**hat do you
think of Dracula films?
Fangtastic!

586 **W**ho brings the monsters their babies?
Frankenstork!

587 **W**hy are ghosts cowards?
Because they've got no guts!

588 **W**hat do Indian ghosts sleep in?

A creepy tipi!

589 **D**id you hear about the ghouls' favorite hotel?

It had running rot and mould!

590 **W**ho speaks at the ghosts' press conference?

The spooksperson!

591 **W**hat is Count Dracula's favorite snack?

A fangfurter!

592 **W**hat do ghosts eat for breakfast?

Dreaded wheat!

593 **W**hat is a ghost's favorite dessert?

Boo-Berry pie with I-scream!

594 **W**hy are graveyards so noisy?

Because of all the coffin!

595 **W**hat do you get if you cross a ghost with a packet of chips?

Snacks that go crunch in the night!

596 **H**ow does a witch tell the time?

With a witch watch!

597 **W**hy did the witch put her broom in the washing machine?

She wanted a clean sweep!

598 **W**hat do you call two witches that share a room?

Broom mates!

599 **W**hat noise does a witch's breakfast cereal make?

Snap, cackle and pop!

Riddles

600 **W**hat dance do hippies hate?

A square dance.

601 **W**hat can be caught and heard, but never seen?

A remark.

602 **W**hat part of a fish weighs the most?

The scales.

603 **W**hat's gray and can't see well from either end?

A donkey with its eyes shut.

604 **W**hat is bigger when it's upside down?

The number 6.

605 **W**hy don't bananas get lonely?

Because they hang around in bunches.

Man...that dance is just so SQUARE! You gotta start thinking in HEXAGONS, man... HEXAGONS

606 **W**hat's the difference between a joke and a wise guy?

One is funny, and one thinks he's funny.

607 **W**hy did the girl keep a ruler on her newspaper?

Because she wanted to get the story straight.

URRGHH
Ever tried to hold a newspaper in one hand and put a ruler on it with the other to get the story straight?

608 **I**f a woman is born in China, grows up in Australia, goes to live in America and dies in New Orleans, what is she?

Dead.

No, no, not thanks. It's THANK-EWE!

609 **W**hat do well-behaved young lambs say to their mothers?

"Thank ewe!"

610 **W**hat has a hundred limbs but cannot walk?

A tree.

611 **H**ow can you tell an undertaker?

By his grave manner.

612 **W**hat can you serve, but never eat?

A tennis ball.

613 **I**f a horse loses its tail, where could it get another?

At a re-tail store.

614 **W**hat goes through water but doesn't get wet?

A ray of light.

615 **T**hree men were in a boat. It capsized, but only two got their hair wet. Why?

The third man was bald!

616 **W**hat do elephants play marbles with?

Old bowling balls.

617 **W**hy do doctors wear masks when operating?

Because if they make a mistake, no one will know who did it!

618 **W**hy did the girl buy a set of tools?

Everyone said she had a screw loose.

619 **W**hy is a bride always out of luck on her wedding day?

Because she never marries the best man.

620 **W**hen Adam introduced himself to Eve, what three words did he use which read the same backward and forward?

"Madam, I'm Adam."

621 **W**hy is a ladies' belt like a garbage truck?

Because it goes around and around to gather the waist.

622 **W**hat is the difference between a hungry person and a greedy person?

One longs to eat, and the other eats too long.

623 **W**hat's the difference between an oak tree and a tight shoe?

One makes acorns, the other makes corns ache.

624 **W**hat is the best cure for dandruff?

Baldness.

625 **W**hat did the dentist say to the golfer?

"You've got a hole in one!"

626 **W**hat does every girl have that she can always count on?

Fingers.

627 **W**hen a boy falls into the water, what is the first thing he does?

Gets wet.

628 **W**hat happened when the snowman had a fight with his girlfriend?

She gave him the cold shoulder.

629 **W**hat do you call a man who doesn't have all his fingers on one hand?

Normal. You have fingers on both hands!

630 **W**hat happened to the horse that swallowed the dollar?

He bucked.

If you've bucked like that after swallowing a DOLLAR, what would you do if you swallowed a CREDIT CARD?

631 **W**hat did one angel say to the other angel?

Halo.

632 **W**hat does a girl look for but hopes she'll never find?

A hole in her pantyhose.

Oh no, there's a hole in my pantyhose!

633 **W**hat trees do fortune tellers prefer?

Palms.

634 **W**hat did Cinderella say when her photos weren't ready?

"Some day my prints will come."

635 **W**hy did the Invisible Man's wife understand him so well?

Because she could see right through him.

636 **W**hy can't anyone stay angry with actors?

Because they always make up.

637 **W**hy was the mother flea so sad?

Because her children were going to the dogs.

638 **W**hy did the boy laugh after his operation?

Because the doctor put him in stitches.

639 If everyone bought a white car, what would we have?

A white carnation.

640 What is a forum?

One-um plus three-um.

641 Why do we dress baby girls in pink and baby boys in blue?

Because babies can't dress themselves.

Obviously radical babies

642 What did the burglar say to the lady who caught him stealing her silver?

"I'm at your service, ma'am."

Now that's my sort of man! "Mr. October"

OCTOBER

643 Why did the girl tear the calendar?

Because she wanted to take a month off.

644 Why didn't the boy go to work in the wool factory?

Because he was too young to dye.

645 **W**hen is a
chair like a
woman's
dress?

When it's satin.

646 **W**hy did the
boy put his
bed in the
fireplace?

*So he could sleep
like a log.*

647 **W**hen does a
timid girl turn
to stone?

When she becomes a little bolder (boulder)!

648 **W**hy did the
boy sit on his
watch?

*He wanted to be
on time.*

649 **W**hat did
Santa Claus'
wife say
during a
thunderstorm?

*"Come and look
at the rain,
Dear."*

650 **W**hat kind of star wears sunglasses?

A movie star.

I know it's 3.30 AM teddy, but I need the sunglasses. It's all part of my movie star image.

651 **W**hy are good intentions like people who faint?

They need carrying out.

652 **W**hat do you call a man who shaves 30 times a day?

A barber.

653 **"D**o these stairs take you to the third floor?"

"No, I'm afraid you'll have to walk!"

654 **W**hat did the mother sardine say to her baby when they saw a submarine?

"Don't be scared. It's only a can of people."

Is that your stomach growling?

No.... not mine!

655 **W**hy is an island like the letter T?

Because it's in the middle of water.

656 **W**hat is the fiercest flower in the garden?

The tiger lily.

657 **W**hat is higher without the head than with it?

A pillow.

658 **W**ho was the fastest runner in the whole world?

Adam, because he was the first in the human race.

659 **W**hat kind of song can you sing in the car?

A car tune!

660 **H**ow does a boat show its affection?

By hugging the shore.

661 **W**hen do clocks die?

When their time's up.

662 **W**hat did the buffalo say to his son when he went away on a long trip?

"Bison."

663 **C**an a match box?

No, but a tin can!

School

A bit of geography ...

664 **W**hat are the names of the small rivers that run into the Nile?

The juve-niles.

665 **W**hat do you know about the Dead Sea?

Dead? I didn't even know it was sick!

666 **W**hy is the Mississippi such an unusual river?

It has four eyes and can't even see.

Gee...the Mississippi really does have four eyes!

667 **W**here is the English Channel?

Not sure. It's not on my T.V.

668 Why does the Statue of Liberty stand in New York harbor?

Because it can't sit down.

The Statue of Liberty must have gotten tired and sat down.

669 Name an animal that lives on the tundra.

A reindeer.

Name another.

Another reindeer.

I reckon I'm hot on this guy's trail!

670 Do you know where to find elephants?

Elephants don't need finding. They're so big they don't get lost.

671 What fur do we get from a tiger?

As fur as possible.

672 What birds are found in Portugal?

Portu-geese.

673 **N**ame three famous poles.

North, south, and tad.

674 **W**hat do you do with crude oil?

Teach it some manners.

General

675 **W**hat do you call someone who greets you at the school door every morning?

Matt.

676 **D**id you hear about the student who said he couldn't write an essay about goldfish because he didn't have any waterproof ink?

677 **H**ave you heard about the gym teacher who ran around exam rooms, hoping to jog students' memories?

678 . . . Or, the home economics teacher who had her pupils in stitches?

679 . . . Or, maybe, the home economics teacher who thought Hamlet was an omelette with bacon?

680 **W**hat would you get if you crossed a teacher with a vampire?

Lots of blood tests.

681 **T**eacher: *"I hope I didn't see you copying from John's exam paper, James."*

James: *"I hope you didn't see me either!"*

682 **F**ather: *"How do you like going to school?"*

Son: *"Going and coming home are fine; it's the part in the middle I don't like!"*

683 **"O**ur teacher talks to herself in class. Does yours?"

"Yes, but she doesn't realize it. She thinks we're listening!"

684 **T**eacher: *"Be sure to go straight home after school."*

Student: *"I can't. I live around the corner!"*

685 **L**augh, and the class laughs with you.

But you get detention alone.

686 **W**hy did the student stand on his head?

To turn things over in his mind.

687 **S**tudent: *"Where can I find out about ducks?"*

Librarian: *"Try the ducktionary."*

688 **M**other: *"I told you not to eat cake before supper."*

Son: *"But it's part of my homework, see: If you take an eighth of a cake from a whole cake, how much is left?"*

Teachers

689 Teacher: *"Why can't you answer any of my questions in class?"*

Student: *"If I could, there wouldn't be much point in me being here."*

690 Teacher: *"What came after the Stone Age and the Bronze Age?"*

Student: *"The saus-age."*

691 Teacher: *"What family does the octopus belong to?"*

Student: *"Nobody's I know."*

692 Why did the teacher wear sunglasses?

Because his students were so bright.

693 Did you hear about the cross-eyed teacher?

He couldn't control his pupils.

694 Teacher: *"What's the name of a liquid that won't freeze?"*

Student: *"Hot water."*

One of those stale old bargain buns that made it's way into the teacher's lunchbox

695 Teacher: *"If I bought 100 buns for a dollar, what would each bun be?"*

Student: *"Old and stale."*

696 Teacher: *"Can anyone tell me what the Dog Star is?"*
Student: *"Lassie."*

Now students... I'm going to turn myself into...

sub-atomic particles

697 Did you hear about the technology teacher who left teaching to try to make something of himself?

698 Parent: *"In my day we didn't have computers at school to help us."*

Child: *"You mean you got your schoolwork wrong all on your own?"*

699 How do you make seven an even number?
Take off the s.

148

700 **D**id you hear
about the math
teacher who
wanted to order
pizza for dinner,
but was divided
about whether
to add more
cheese?

Here's your ·74 share of the entire pizza with 0·25% extra cheese!

701 **W**hat do you get if you cross a homeroom teacher
and a traffic cop?

*Someone who gives you 500 double yellow lines for being
late.*

702 **W**hat is an English teacher's favorite fruit?

The Grapes of Wrath.

*A rainy night...
A dinner party...
Salmon dip...
A Butler...
All adds up to a
murder to me*

703 **W**hy are math
teachers good
at solving
detective
stories?

*They're quick at
adding up clues.*

704 **W**hat is the
easiest way to
get a day off
school?

*Wait until
Saturday.*

705 **W**hat is the robot's favorite part of school?

Assembly.

706 **H**ow many letters are in the alphabet?

Eleven. Count them -t-h-e-a-l-p-h-a-b-e-t!

707 **W**hy can you believe everything a bearded teacher tells you?

They can't tell bald-faced lies.

708 **D**id you hear about the two history teachers who were dating?

They go to restaurants to talk about old times.

709 **D**id you hear about the teacher who wore sunglasses to give out exam results?

He took a dim view of his students' performance.

710 **H**ow does a math teacher know how long she sleeps?

She takes a ruler to bed.

711 **W**hat type of instruments did the early Britons play?

The Anglo-saxophone.

712 **W**hat do you call an art teacher who is always complaining?

Mona Lisa.

713 **T**eacher: *"Why are you eating candy in my classroom?"*
Ed: *"Because the shop had run out of gum."*

714 **W**hat word is always spelled wrong?

Wrong.

715 **M**ath teacher: *"Anne, why have you brought a picture of the queen of England with you today?"*

Anne: *"You told us to bring a ruler with us."*

716 **M**ath teacher: *"Richard, if you had 50 cents in each pants pocket, and $2 in each jacket pocket, what would you have?"*

Richard: *"Someone else's clothes, Sir."*

717 **W**hat kind of tests do witch teachers give?

Hex-aminations.

718 **S**tudent: *"I don't think I deserve a zero on this test."*

Teacher: *"Neither do I, but it was the lowest I could give you!"*

719 **T**eacher: *"Jessica, you aren't paying attention to me. Are you having trouble hearing?"*

Jessica: *"No, I'm having trouble listening."*

720 **T**eacher: *"You missed school yesterday, didn't you?"*

Student: *"Not very much."*

721 **S**tudent: *"I didn't do my homework because I lost my memory."*

Teacher: *"When did this start?"*

Student: *"When did what start?"*

722 **P**laying truant from school is like having a credit card.

Lots of fun now, pay later.

723 **T**eacher: *"Why didn't you answer me, Stuart?"*

Stuart: *"I did. I shook my head."*

Teacher: *"You don't expect me to hear it rattling from here, do you?"*

724 **W**hy was the principal worried?

Because there were so many rulers in the school.

725 **T**eacher: *"I told you to stand at the end of the line."*

Student: *"I tried, but someone was already there."*

726 **T**eacher: *"I told you to draw a cow eating grass, but you've only drawn a cow."*

Student: *"The cow has eaten all the grass."*

727 **T**eacher: *"Why haven't you been to school for the past two weeks, Billy?"*

Billy: *"It's not my fault. Whenever I go to cross the road outside, there's a man with a sign saying 'Stop Children Crossing'!"*

728 **D**id you hear about the teacher who locked the school band in a deep freeze?

They wanted to play really cool jazz.

729 Teacher: *"What bird doesn't build its own nest?"*

Student: *"The cuckoo."*

Teacher: *"That's right. How did you know that?"*

Student: *"Everyone knows cuckoos live in clocks!"*

730 History teacher: *"Why were ancient sailing ships so eco-friendly?"*

Student: *"Because they could go for hundreds of miles to the galleon."*

731 Math teacher: *"If you multiplied 1,386 by 395, what would you get?"*

Student: *"The wrong answer."*

732 Why did the boy throw his watch out of the window during a test?

Because he wanted to make time fly.

733 **E**nglish teacher: *"James, give me a sentence with the word 'counterfeit' in it."*

James: *"I wasn't sure if she was a centipede or a millipede, so I had to count her feet."*

734 **C**omputer teacher: *"Sarah, give me an example of software."*

Sarah: *"A floppy hat."*

735 **"W**hat were you before you started school, girls and boys?"* asked the teacher, hoping that someone would say *"babies"*.

She was disappointed when all the children cried out, *"Happy!"*

736 **T**eacher: *"That's the stupidest boy in the whole school."*

Mother: *"That's my son."*

Teacher: *"Oh! I'm so sorry."*

Mother: *"You're sorry?"*

737 **M**y teacher says I have such bad handwriting that I ought to be a doctor!

738 "I hope you're not one of those boys who sits and watches the school clock," said the principal to the new boy.

"No, Sir," he replied. "I have a digital watch that beeps at 3:15!"

739 Ben's teacher thinks Ben is a wonder child.

She wonders whether he'll ever learn anything.

740 "How old would you say I am, Francis?" the teacher asked.

"Forty," said the boy promptly.

"What makes you think I'm 40?" asked the puzzled teacher.

"My big brother is 20," he replied, "and you're twice as silly as he is!"

741 "I'm not going to school today," said Alexander to his mother. "The teachers bully me and the boys don't like me."

"That's not too surprising. You're 35 years old," replied his mother, "and you're the principal!"

742 *"What do you like about your new school, Billy?"* asked Uncle Ned.

"When it's closed!"

743 First teacher: *"What's wrong with young Jimmy today? I saw him running around the playground, screaming and pulling at his hair."*

Second teacher: *"Don't worry. He's just lost his marbles."*

Gee...I'd hate to see what he'd do if he lost his school bag instead of his marbles!

744 Simple Simon was writing a geography essay for his teacher. It began like this:

The people who live in Paris are called parasites . . .

Quick Wanda! Take a photo before it bites... it's a PARASITE

USA

A-Z PARIS

745 Teacher: *"Are you good at arithmetic?"*
Mary: *"Well, yes and no."*
Teacher: *"What do you mean, yes and no?"*
Mary: *"Yes, I'm no good at arithmetic."*

746 Home economics teacher: *"Joe, what are the best things to put in a chocolate cake?"*
Joe: *"Teeth!"*

I don't like nuts in my chocolate cake...or teeth either... ...for that matter.

747 Teacher: *"Your daughter's only 5 and she can spell her name backwards? Why, that's remarkable!"*
Mother: *"Yes, we're very proud of her."*
Teacher: *"And what is your daughter's name?"*
Mother: *"Anna."*

748 **"W**hat are three words most often used by students?"* the teacher asked the class.
"I don't know," sighed a student.
"That's correct!" said the teacher.

749 Shane: *"Dad, today my teacher yelled at me for something I didn't do."*
Dad: *"What did he yell at you for?"*
Shane: *"For not doing my homework."*

750 Teacher: *"If you had one dollar and asked your dad for one dollar, how much money would you have?"*

Student: *"One dollar."*

Teacher: *"Are you sure?"*

Student: *"Yes, my dad wouldn't give me a dollar."*

751 Teacher: *"Billy, stop making ugly faces at the other students!"*

Billy: *"Why?"*

Teacher: *"When I was your age, I was told that if I kept making ugly faces, my face would stay that way."*

Billy: *"Well, I can see you didn't listen."*

Silly Book Titles

752 *My Golden Wedding* by Annie Versary

753 *The Terrible Problem* by Major Setback

754 *A Load of Old Rubbish* by Stephan Nonsense

755 *Tape Recording for Beginners* by Cass Ette

756 *Don't Leave Without Me* by Isa Coming

Gee... This stuff really works

ONCE AND FOR ALL DANDRUFF LOTION

Every igloo starts with the first block of ice

Please empty me.

LITTER

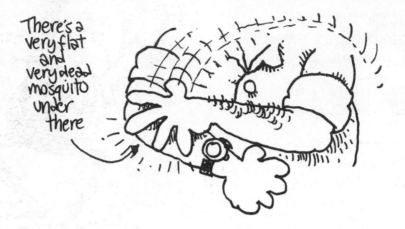

SQUARE DANCING

Hi...I'm new at this ...but the note says... HAND OVER ALL YOUR CASH!

You want I.D. Is a driver's license OK?

TELLER 2

QUEUE HERE

A GHOST OF A WITCH

836 *Winning the Lottery* by Jack Potts

837 *Robbers Who Got Away With It* by Hugh Dunnit

838 *Classic Furniture* by Ann Teaks

839 *Keeping Pet Snakes* by Sir Pent

840 *The Omen* by B. Warned

841 *Mean Cats* by Claude Bottom

842 *The Bad Tempered Werewolf* by Claudia Armoff

Space

868 **W**hy did the boy become an astronaut?

Because he had his head in the stars.

869 **W**hat creates the most housework in alien homes?

Stardust.

870 **W**here do astronauts leave their space ships?

At parking meteors!

871 **W**hat do you call the bugs on the moon?

Luna-tics

872 **H**ow do you get a baby astronaut to sleep?

You rock-et!

873 **W**hat's an astronaut's favorite game?

Moonopoly!

874 **H**ow do spacemen pass the time on long trips?

They play astronauts and crosses!

875 **W**hy does meat taste better in space?

Because it's meteor!

876 **W**hy did Captain Kirk go into the ladies' toilet?

To boldly go where no man has gone before!

877 **F**irst astronaut: *"I'm hungry."*

Second astronaut: *"So am I. It must be launch time."*

878 **C**an I have a return ticket to the moon please?

Sorry the moon's full tonight.

879 **W**hat do you call a space magician?

A flying sorcerer!

880 **"I** want to be an astronaut when I grow up."

"What high hopes you have!"

881 **W**hat do you call an overweight E.T.?

An extra cholesterol.

882 **W**hat did the metric alien say?

"Take me to your liter!"

883 **W**hat did the alien say to the gas pump?

"Don't you know it's rude to stick your finger in your ear?"

884 **H**ow does a robot alien shave?

With a laser blade!

885 **W**hat do you call a robot who takes the longest route?

R2 Detour!

886 **W**hat holds the moon up?

Moonbeams!

Sport

887 **W**hat job does Dracula have with the Transylvanian baseball team?

He's the bat boy.

888 **W**hy is bowling the quietest sport?

Because you can hear a pin drop.

889 **"I** can't see us ever finishing this bowling game."

"Why is that?"

"Every time I knock all the pins down, someone calls a strike!"

Now when you get out there... I want to see HOME RUNS from you guys!

890 **W**hat part of a football field smells the best?

The scenter spot!

891 **W**hy aren't football stadiums built in outer-space?

Because there is no atmosphere!

892 **W**hich goalkeeper can jump higher than a crossbar?

All of them. A crossbar can't jump!

893 **W**hy did the soccer star hold his shoe to his ear?

Because he liked sole music!

I dig that grooovy sole music!

I think these NUTS support some South American football team!

GO BRAZIL!

894 **W**hat are Brazilian soccer fans called?

Brazil nuts!

895 **W**here do football players dance?

At a foot ball!

896 **W**hat sort of nails do you find in football shoes?

Toenails.

897 **W**hat lights up a football stadium?

A good football game!

898 **H**ow do you start a doll's race?

Ready, Teddy, Go!

899 **W**hy wouldn't the coach let elephants on the swim team?

He was afraid they would drop their trunks.

900 **H**ow do hens encourage their favorite basketball teams?

They egg them on!

901 **W**ho won the race between two balls of string?

They were tied!

902 **H**ow did the basketball court get wet?

The players dribbled all over it!

903 **W**hy don't grasshoppers go to baseball games?

They prefer a game of cricket.

904 **W**hy didn't the dog want to play football?

It was a boxer!

905 **W**hy does a polo player ride a horse?

Because they're too heavy to carry.

906 **H**ow do you stop squirrels from playing football in the yard?

Hide the ball, it drives them nuts!

907 **W**hy should you be careful when playing against a team of big cats?

They might be cheetahs!

908 **W**hy do football coaches bring suitcases along to away games?

So that they can pack the defense!

909 **N**ame a tennis player's favorite city.

Volley Wood

910 **W**hy was the team manager shaking the cat?

To see if there was any money in the kitty!

911 **W**here do football coaches go when they are sick of the game?

The bored room!

912 **C**oach: *"I thought I told you to lose weight. What happened to your three week diet?"*

Player: *"I finished it in three days!"*

913 **C**oach: *"Our new player cost $10 million. I call him our wonder player."*

Fan: *"Why's that?"*

Coach: *"Every time he plays, I wonder why I bothered to draft him!"*

914 **C**oach: *"I'll give you $100 a week to start, and $500 a week in a year."*

Baseball player: *"See you in a year!"*

915 **W**hat happens when an athlete gets angry with his computer?

He becomes a floppy diskus thrower.

916 **W**hy aren't turkeys allowed to play football?

Because they always use fowl language.

917 **W**here do old bowling balls end up?

In the gutter!

918 **W**hy do artists never win when they play basketball?

They keep drawing the foul!

919 **W**hat did they call Dracula when he refereed the World Series?

The Vumpire!

920 **W**hy does someone who runs marathons make a good student?

Because education pays off in the long run!

921 **W**hat is a runner's favorite subject in school?

Jog-raphy!

922 **W**hat stories do basketball players tell?

Tall tales!

Crazy Fools

923 **D**id you hear about the fool who hijacked a submarine?

He demanded $2 dollars and a parachute.

924 **W**hy did the crazy sailor grab some soap when his ship sank?

Because he thought he would wash ashore.

925 **D**id you hear about the crazy sailor who was discharged from his submarine duties?

He was found sleeping with the window open.

926 **A** crazy bank robber rushes into a bank, points two fingers at the teller and says,

"This is a muckup."

"Don't you mean a stickup?" said the teller.

"No. It's a muckup," replied the robber. *"I've forgotten my gun!"*

927 **"S**o you took your medicine right after your bath?" the doctor asked his crazy patient.

"No, doctor," replied the fool.

"By the time I'd drunk the bath, I had no room left for the medicine!"

928 **D**id you hear about the crazy cyclist who won the Tour de France?

He did a lap of honor.

929 **W**hy did the team of fools always lose the tug-of-war?

They pushed.

930 **D**id you hear about the foolish karate champion who joined the army?

The first time he saluted, he nearly killed himself.

931 **T**he teacher told the crazy fool she knew he'd skipped school last Friday, and heard he'd been playing games at the arcade.

The fool told her it wasn't true — and he had the baseball game tickets to prove it!

932 **H**ow does a fool call his dog?

He puts two fingers in his mouth and shouts "Rover!"

933 **T**he fool saw a sign outside a police station that read *Man Wanted For Robbery*, and went in and applied for the job!

934 **D**id you hear about the crazy photographer?

He saved used light bulbs for his dark room.

935 **H**ave you heard about the fool who thinks a fjord is a Scandinavian motor car?

936 **W**hen the fool's co-worker asked why he had a sausage stuck behind his ear, he replied, *"Oh… I must have eaten my pencil for lunch!"*

937 **T**he gang's boss was surprised to find one of his gang sawing the legs off his bed.

"Why are you doing that?" he asked.

"Well, you did ask me to lie low for a bit," the fool replied.

938 *"Y*our finger is in my soup bowl!" said the man.

"Don't worry," said the foolish waiter. *"The soup isn't hot."*

My left thumb thinks It's Cream of Chicken ...my right thinks It's Pumpkin.

939 **S**usie asked the fool if his tent leaked when he was on vacation.

"Only when it rained," he said.

A perfect landing

WALLY-AIR

940 **W**hy did the crazy pilot land his plane on a house?

Because the homeowner had left the landing lights on.

941 *"A*re you lost?" the policeman asked the foolish schoolgirl.

"Of course not," she replied. *"I'm here, it's my school that's lost."*

942 **D**id you hear about the crazy hitchhiker?

He got up early so there wouldn't be much traffic around.

943 **H**ave you heard about the fool who went into a store open 24 hours and asked what time they closed?

What do you call

944 . . . a fairy who never takes a bath?

Stinkerbell!

945 . . . a man with a paper bag on his head?

Russell!

946 . . . a man with a seagull on his head?

Cliff!

947 . . . a man who had an accident?

Derek!

948 . . . a man with a map on his head?

Miles!

949 . . . a flying policeman?

Heli-copper!

950 . . . a carrot who talked back to the cook?

A fresh vegetable!

951 . . . a skunk in a courthouse?

Odor in the court!

952 . . . the chief's daughter when she's in trouble?

Miss Chief!

953 . . . a man with a large black and blue mark on his head?

Bruce!

954 . . . a man with some cat scratches on his head?

Claude!

955 . . . an egg laid by a dog?

A pooched egg!

956 . . . a boy with an encyclopedia in his pants?
Smarty pants.

957 . . . a train full of gum?
A chew chew train!

958 . . . a woman standing in a breeze?
Gail!

The new season's windswept look

959 . . . a woman with a tortoise on her head?
Shelley!

960 . . . a cat that joined the Red Cross?
A first aid kit!

MEOW . . .

FIRST AID KIT

961 . . . a rabbit locked in a sauna?
A hot cross bunny!

962 . . . a man with a legal document?
Will!

963 . . . a man with a truck on his head?
Deceased!

Wicked

964 **"D**addy, can I have another glass of water, please?"

"Okay, but that's the twelfth one I've given you tonight."

"Yes I know, but my bedroom is still on fire."

965 **W**hat's the difference between school lunches and a pile of slugs?

School lunches are on plates.

966 **J**ohn: *"Do you know anyone who has gone on the television?"*

Wendy: *"Just my dog, but he's housetrained now."*

967 **D**id you hear about the two fat men who ran a marathon?

One ran in short bursts, the other ran in burst shorts.

968 **W**hy are naughty kids like maggots?

Because they try to wriggle out of everything.

969 **A** woman woke her husband in the middle of the night.

"There's a burglar in the kitchen eating the cake I made!" she said.

"Who should I call?" asked her husband. "The police or an ambulance?"

970 **M**y cousin spent a bundle on deodorant, until he found out people just didn't like him . . .

971 **D**id you hear about the two bodies cremated at the same time?

It was a dead heat.

972 **D**id you hear about the dentist who became a brain surgeon?

His drill slipped.

973 What did they prove when the steam roller ran over the man?

That he had lots of guts.

974 Boy: *"Dad there's a black cat in the dining room!"*

Dad: *"That's okay son, black cats are lucky."*

Son: *"This one is — he's eating your dinner!"*

975 The cruise ship passenger was feeling really seasick, when the waiter asked if he'd like some lunch.

"No thanks," he replied.

"Just throw it over the side and save me the trouble."

976 **A** mushroom walks onto the playground and asks *"Can I play?"*

But the other kids refuse.

The mushroom says, *"Why not? I'm a fun-gi!"*

977 **H**airdresser: "Would you like a haircut?"

Boy: "No, I'd like them all cut."

978 **S**he's so ugly that when a wasp stings her, it has to shut its eyes!

979 A man out for a walk came across a little boy pulling his cat's tail.

"Hey you!" he shouted. *"Don't pull the cat's tail!"*

"I'm not pulling," replied the boy. *"I'm only holding on. The cat's doing the pulling!"*

980 There's no point in telling some people a joke with a double meaning.

They wouldn't understand either of them!

981 George is the type of boy that his mother doesn't want him to hang around with . . .

982 Three guys, Shutup, Manners, and Poop, were walking down the road when Poop fell down. Shutup went to get help. He found a policeman who asked, *"What's your name?"*

"Shutup," he answered.

"Hey, where are your manners!" the policeman exclaimed.

Shutup replied, *"Outside on the road, picking up Poop!"*

983 Three girls walked into a beauty shop. Two had blonde hair and one had green hair. The stylist asked the blondes, *"How did you get to be blonde?"*

"Oh, it's natural," they replied.

The stylist asked the other girl, *"How did your hair become green?"*

She replied, *"Rub your hand on your nose and then across your hair."*

984 **F**ather: *"Johnny got an A on his assignment! I think he got his brains from me."*

Mother: *"I think you're right. I've still got mine."*

985 **S**am: *"Mom, can I have a pony for Christmas?"*

Mom: *"Of course not. You'll have turkey just like the rest of us."*

986 **A** man went into a cafe and ordered two slices of apple pie with four scoops of ice cream, covered with whipped cream and piled high with chopped nuts.

"Would you like a cherry on top?" asked the waitress.

"No thanks," said the man. *"I'm on a diet."*

987 **D**avey: *"Dad, there's a man at the door collecting for a new swimming pool."*

Dad: *"Alright, give him a glass of water."*

988 **H**ave you ever seen a man-eating tiger?

No, but in a restaurant I once saw a man eating chicken.

989 **W**hat do you get when an elephant stands on your roof?

Mushed rooms.

990 **A** man came running out of his house as the garbage truck was driving by.

Man: *"Did I miss the garbage collection?"*

Garbage man: *"No, jump in."*

991 **W**hat did the dragon say when he saw the knight in his shining armor?

"Oh no! Not more canned food!"

992 **W**hat do you get when you cross a vampire with an elf?

A monster that sucks blood out of people's kneecaps.

993 **W**hat did the monster do when he lost a hand?

He went to the second-hand shop.

994 **W**here would you get a job playing an elastic trumpet?

In a rubber band!

995 **W**hat is a volcano?

A mountain with the hiccups.

996 **W**hat goes in many different colors but always comes out blue?

A swimmer on a cold day!

997 **W**hy does the ocean roar?

Because there are oysters in its bed!

998 **W**hat do you call a one-legged woman?

Eileen!

999 **W**hose fault is it when an ax hits a car?

No one's, it's an ax-ident.

1000 One Sunday morning, a little old lady saw a boy walking through the park carrying a fishing pole and a jar of tadpoles.

"*Young man,*" she said. "*You shouldn't be going fishing on a Sunday?*"

"*I'm not going fishing, Ma'am,*" he called back. "*I'm going home!*"

1001 A man was on a full subway, when a giant lady next to him said, "*If you were a gentleman, you'd stand up and let someone else sit down.*"

The man replied, "*And if you were a lady, you'd stand up and let four people sit down.*"